I0560093

Travis I. Sivart

27 Thoughts About Steampunk

Travis I. Sivart

Travis I. Sivart

27 Thoughts About Steampunk
27 Thoughts on Social DIY Series, Book 1

Copyright © 2016 Travis I. Sivart

Cover Design by Travis I. Sivart

ISBN: 978-1-954214-42-2

Talk of the Tavern Publishing Group

Talk of the Tavern
Publishing Group

Travis I. Sivart

Dedication

This book is dedicated to all those great folks who I met at countless events, conventions, parties, online, and so many other places, and who love steampunk as much as I do.

Travis I. Sivart

Table of Contents

Introduction

This book is just what it says, 27 thoughts on steampunk. It's the beginning of a much larger conversation, and is meant to open the floodgates of ideas and pique your interest, and perhaps explain a few things in simple terms.

It isn't a definitive tome of knowledge of all things steampunk. If you want something that covers more...I recommend you take a look at the book which I wrote with Wendy L. Callahan, *Steampunk For Simpletons: A Fun Primer For Folks Who Aren't Sure What Steampunk Is All About.*

My experience in steampunk comes from attending steampunk events and conventions as a speaker and author, running an online steampunk radio show, writing steampunk short stories and novels, and just loving the genre. I don't know it all, but I have experienced a lot.

I try to cover the same things I often talk about when meeting someone who is discovering steampunk for the first time. I hope it helps you begin an exciting journey into a rich and fascinating hobby.

Travis I. Sivart

1. What Steampunk Is

Many people like to use words like Retro-futurism or Neo-Victorian to define steampunk. I don't know if those words help or just create more confusion. In the simplest terms, steampunk is Victorian era style, with high technology that is usually steam based as a method of functioning.

Steampunk is an aesthetic of style, fashion, manners, and mindset that are largely drawn from the age of the English Queen, Victoria, thus the Victorian Era. It draws upon science fiction writers from the nineteenth century as inspiration of what the world could have been, with a dash of time travel thrown in for a good measure.

It goes hand in hand with the mindset of recycling the old for new, and repurposing things whose original uses have been lost. It embraces the blending and combining of different things to create something greater and unique.

Travis I. Sivart

2. Where Steampunk Came From

Depending on your point of view and mindset, Steampunk could have come from a few different places. In the most modern terms, author K.W. Jeter coined the phrase in an interview with Lotus Magazine in 1989. But its roots go much further back. Some would say at least a hundred years. I can show a steampunk influence all the way back to ancient Greece.

Most would agree that it largely was born in the minds and writings of the grandfathers of science fiction, Jules Verne and H.G. Wells. I would include the grandmother of science fiction, Mary Shelley, famous for *Frankenstein*, which was published nearly a half-century before Verne published his first work.

Others would point to more modern roots in works like K.W. Jeter's *Infernal Devices* (1987) and William Gibson's *The Difference Engine* (1990), or even in comic books such as *The League of Extraordinary Gentlemen* (1999). By the time the movie remake of *Wild, Wild, West* with Will Smith (1999) based on the 1965 television series came out, steampunk had a firm standing as its own genre.

Travis I. Sivart

3. Genre or Aesthetic

Many discussions on this topic have occurred. Many say it is a genre, but I would say they haven't looked deep enough. It has the feel of a genre when applied to a single movie or fashion, but in truth, it's much more profound than that. A genre isn't a large enough thing to hold and define steampunk. This thing we've created can be applied to fashion, style, décor, movies, books, and more. As an aesthetic, you can take anything and give it a steampunk flavor, flair, or feel.

Music, movies, and more have all used the seasoning of steampunk to make their fare more palatable by peppering their productions with the elements that make steampunk unique. Steampunk is the only genre that doesn't have a base example, in fact, quite the opposite. The fashions, movies, and more that are steampunk are following the steampunk crowd rather than us looking to media for how to do it. We created it and are constantly recreating and redefining it in everything we do.

Travis I. Sivart

4. History's Influence

We draw heavily from the Victorian Era. The Victorian era of British history was the period of Queen Victoria's reign from June 20th, 1837, until her death, on January 22nd, 1901. We take our favorite bits of that era's fashion and style, blend it with the manners, women's rights movements, equal rights roots, age of discovery and exploration in science, medicine, and more and make something that is our own.

We add in details from fictional characters like Sherlock Holmes, gothic horror and magic, scientists like Tesla, and more, and make something that stands out from the dark history that is reality. But that history is there, and it's a powerful influence.

Others go further still, and draw from their favorite periods of history outside of the standards mentioned above. This is easily done with steampunk, due to time travel, and is quite acceptable and even encouraged.

I've seen togas, chain mail armor, halberds, muskets, flintlocks, cartouches, Tommy guns, and so much more from different time periods in Earth's history.

Travis I. Sivart

5. Modern Steampunk

Modern media has laced the steampunk influence into art and fashion many times, even appearing in the holiday décor of many top name department stores or the styles of top fashion designers. It has appeared in dozens of movies, books, songs, and more.

One beautiful thing that steampunk encourages is multi-culturism. The acceptance of different cultures, even the blending of them. It inspires us to see the beauty of our differences, and embrace the chance to learn something new or share our own unique backgrounds with others. It discourages judging others based on them being different. Instead, we discover new things.

It also allows genre mashing. I have seen steampunk superheroes, steampunk Star Wars and Star Trek, Romans in togas with ray guns, and explorers from other worlds wearing sneakers and jeans. Anime has also brought a lot of steampunk into its fold.

Travis I. Sivart

6. Time Travel

One thing that allows steampunk to blend so many things into itself is the concept of time travel. H.G. Wells wrote The Time Machine, and many other steampunk authors, then and now, include time travel in their works. Though this is often based on characters from the Victorian Era, it lets you bring any time into your world as you conceive it.

You can have a smart phone but be in full renaissance garb. You can bring anime characters, hard sci-fi, and so much more into your costumes and concepts.

Time travel also allows people dressed in different eras' styles to interact with reasonable familiarity if role-playing, (I'll tell you more about that later), or just let history buffs compare notes and share stories.

Travis I. Sivart

7. Why Punk Works

Punk is about rebellion against the current system. Steampunk rebels with courtesy. It encourages recycling and repurposing, making the old new again, or making the new old again. It encourages creativity in your own personal arena; whether that is costuming, gadgets, storytelling, or trying to make the world a better place by using clean sources of energy.

Steampunk arose in a time when self-centered egotism was reaching a peak. A sense of entitlement was sweeping multiple generations, and a "throwaway" society was becoming the norm. We stand against those things, sometimes indirectly and sometimes directly. We want people to see that we all share this world, and we all need to be responsible for its care and needs. And we need to do this with civility, equality, and poise. That is the punk in steampunk.

Travis I. Sivart

8. Neo-Victorianism & Retro-Futurism

Neo means new, and Victorianism refers to the Victorian era. So Neo-Victorianism is that historical era, by way of all the best parts of it, being renewed. Retro-futurism is making something futuristic by using retro, or old, technology.

These terms make sense once you have a context and understanding of them. Otherwise, they are just fancy words that sound good. It's the knowledge of what they want to convey that makes them inspiring.

Steampunk is renewing the feeling of exploration and discovery, thinking outside of the box, and giving the world an explosion of creativity. With the love and knowledge of the past blended into it, we hope to avoid the mistakes history made, learn from them, and move forward instead.

Travis I. Sivart

9. Authenticity in Steampunk

Some folks demand authenticity in their cosplay or reenactment, even in steampunk. The beauty of steampunk, though, is that the authenticity is strictly based on your own perception and concept. This is a made up mechanism, it's not based on one single thing. It's an amalgamation of many concepts and ideas, becoming one special entity that represents you and your concepts.

Gears and cogs don't have to be practical, they can be decorative. They may represent something that could be functional, but it isn't required. You don't have to have buttons if you prefer zippers. Buttons can be plastic instead of bone or metal, because this is a recreation of an undefined world that sprang from the imagination of thousands of people, who are constantly working together to make something new and old.

10. Playing a Role

Role-playing, it's something that most people have done since they were children, and people have been doing it since time immemorial. It's often referred to as playing pretend or make-believe. Some folks even continue it into their adulthood, pretending to be one person at work and another at home. My point is that this comes as natural as anything else, and should be embraced for the sake of the joy it brings.

If you enjoy dressing up and pretending to be someone else, steampunk is for you. Many of the creative folks in the steampunk community would love to hear your detailed backstory to go with the character and outfit, and share theirs with you. We love to hear the details and reasons behind your fictional history. Are you a noble dandy, an intrepid explorer, a hard working engineer, a lost time traveler, an airship pirate, or something else? We want to know!

Oh, and by the way, if you enjoy dressing up and just being you, steampunk is for you also.

Travis I. Sivart

11. Personal Style

Another draw of steampunk is you can be you, personified. You can take your own personal style and blend it with a concept or outfit and it works.

I love old-fashioned hats, and fedoras are my favorite. I have added them to a few of my outfits, but change it up with Homburgs, boaters, fezzes, bowlers, even Napoleonic Continental Army headgear. The point is that I took one thing that I use in my personal style and used it in my steampunk outfitting.

Do you like torn jeans? Work it into your outfit. Maybe you enjoy a certain style of eye makeup or nail polish; incorporate it. Love being a goth? Well, convert it to steampunk. Proud of your tattoos and piercings? Show them off when you build your outfit.

What about building things? Well, carry the tools of your trade, or the favorite gizmo you made with you wherever you go. I've seen tailors and seamstresses, chefs and cooks, engineers and mechanics, doctors and nurses, cobblers and carpenters, metalworkers and machinists, and so much more, all proudly displaying their tools and wares.

Travis I. Sivart

12. Costuming & Clothing

In steampunk you can dress however you like, but it's primarily Victorian, old west, civil war, or something similar. There are more patterns for making your own clothes available every day as the big companies—such as McCall, Butterick, and Simplicity—realize we love to make things with our own hands. You can also incorporate styles from your ethnic heritage, or adopt from one you adore if you prefer. There is no limit except what you place upon yourself.

You can also buy pre-made clothing without fear of judgement by others. This is a common way to get started—or to up your game once you have the basics—especially if you don't have the time (or perhaps skill) to craft things with your own hands. There are tons of websites where you can buy appropriate clothing.

You can also visit thrift stores to find amazing additions to your collection, though this takes a bit more creativity to put something together. Or you can just raid your own closet (or your grandparents) and find wonderful things there.

Travis I. Sivart

13. Signature Gear

Some folks have a piece of gear or equipment that they become known for, and it identifies them throughout the steampunk community. For some, this may be a huge, towering, custom-built power suit with whirring gears and clicking cogs. As cool as these things can be, you don't have to do that if it isn't your thing.

I have a wonderful piece of signature gear that is a simple leather bracer with an embedded watch, compass, and thermometer. A hinged brass plate covers them. Another signature piece I have is a pin that is a key wrapped with copper wire with a tobacco pipe charm. The last piece I have that I would classify as a signature piece is a leather, sleeveless trench coat. All three of these pieces invite conversation and recognition.

Your signature piece can be jewelry, a gizmo, a hairstyle, tattoos, or anything else. It'll make you recognizable and open up conversations.

Travis I. Sivart

14. Hats & Accessories

Hats, besides ball caps, are essentially a product of bygone eras. Because of this, they make excellent pieces that define an outfit, complete it, or allow it to stand out. They often make people immediately recognize your outfit as something from a different time. I recommend trying different styles and finding something that fits your head and face shape the best, then getting a few to supplement your outfit.

Other accessories do the same. Some I will detail in the next few pages, but some are going to be your own personal flair, style, and discovery. Perhaps it's a walking stick, parasol, book, flask, piece of jewelry, or some other tidbit that you find charming and adds to your outfit.

Travis I. Sivart

15. Hair

Researching hairstyles can be quite rewarding for men or women. It's one more thing that makes you stand apart from our modern style. Whether it's a rockabilly look, a 1930s slick, the ageless hair buns of librarians, or any other, use them.

Hair pins, barrettes, leather wraps, beads, and clips are just a few things you can use to accent the styles and fashions from centuries past. Baby doll curls, bobs, ponytails, and so much more can give you a look that conveys an image from bygone days.

Some men may bellyache that women have so much more diversity in this area, but that is far from true. Men (and a few select women) have the wonders of facial hair to play with. Handlebar moustaches, mutton chops, sideburns, and full beards are just a few of the styles that can be adopted to give you that unique look that will make you stand out in any era!

Travis I. Sivart

16. Goggles & Glasses

Let's face it; goggles have become a staple and recognizable piece of gear associated with steampunk. People add them to every type of attire, from top hats to dirt smudged engineer outfits, from an adventurer's pith helmet to a nest of braids upon a noblewoman's head. As much as I personally feel you should have a reason for wearing a pair, do what you want and make it your own.

And glasses can do the same, especially if you have the kind with the multiple lenses on little brass arms that you can drop in front of your glasses. Or horn rim glasses, reading glasses, wire frames, round lenses, or whatever. Embrace the idea of the high tech and intelligent style that comes with an extra set of eyes!

Travis I. Sivart

17. Parasols, Gloves, & Fans

Did you know there was a secret flirting language associated with parasols, gloves, and fans? All three had their own code, though they were all similar. With a flick of your wrist you could show interest, disdain, tell him to come closer, or to meet you in an hour. It was basic info, but it was enough to get into trouble.

These were mostly the arena of women, but in the modern world there is nothing stopping a man from using the same techniques if it fits you.

On the other hand, pun intended, these items are just fun to have. They make you look and feel a bit classy, out of the era, and they're great for pointing, poking, or waving around in a fit of hysterics. Just be careful with that last one, the period cure for hysterics was a bit risqué!

Travis I. Sivart

18. Bags, Purses, & Satchels

Pockets weren't always as common as they are now. And if you look around, you can find awesome and eclectic bags to fit almost any style. Leather messenger bags, canvas duffels, thigh bags, clutches, or any sort of purse variation can add a lot to your outfit, whether you are a man or woman.

If you like something a bit more masculine or rugged, consider something in canvas or leather, and check out military surplus stores or camping stores for some great options. As always, looking online opens up a literal world of possibilities.

If you want something a bit more delicate and dainty, then look into lace coin purses, clutches, etc. And don't hesitate to create some of your own from PVC, brass hinges, copper wire, a bit of chain, and some spray paint!

Travis I. Sivart

19. Weapons

Weapons can change the whole feel of an outfit, giving you an air of authority, danger, military precision, maniacal insanity, and any number of other attitudes. It allows you to show off the cool historic or imaginative armaments you have.

Weapons can be in any form, from historic replicas to ray guns straight from the pages of science fiction. Many people enjoy carrying swords, daggers, or knives from their favorite bygone era. Others repaint foam dart or water guns to look like retro-futuristic showpieces. And some folks just make crazy things all on their own!

Travis I. Sivart

20. Gizmos & Gadgets

A staple of the steampunk culture is being fun and creative, and having gizmos and gadgets feed right into that. Whether it's a period child's toy of wood and string, or a full body shiny brass doodad, it's just fun to have something cool to show off.

Gizmos and gadgets are really just a broad spectrum term for cool things to fiddle with and show off. They may or may not have an actual function, that's up to you. They can also be made up of brass, wood, wire, paper, cloth, or cobbled together with a variety of medias.

These items can be purchased or self-made. There's no limit to the creativity that can be put into these, the sky's the limit. Searching the internet will reveal a treasure trove of awesome goodies to get some ideas, or to purchase if you aren't able, or interested, in making your own.

Travis I. Sivart

21. Crafting

Making things with your own hands was a fading art, but steampunk is assisting in bringing that back. There's a great feeling when you're using, wearing, or gifting something that you put together with your own hands and creativity.

Sewing, leatherwork, tinkering, building, repurposing, and so many other things fall under the heading of crafting. If you have the sort of mind that allows you to create something from something else, you'll be in your element in steampunk.

There are entire communities on and offline dedicated to sharing ideas, tips, and tricks for making steampunk crafts. It's a great way to share and learn, not to mention making new friends.

Travis I. Sivart

22. Food & Drink

One of the best ways we get to know each other is over a meal or getting together for drinks. Steampunk is no different, except it offers a world full of choices from over a century and a half. Whether it's a modern meal, classic drinks like tea and coffee, sharing a flask, or a full eight-course meal cooked in copper kettles, there are a lot of ways to draw this eternal ritual into the hobby.

I encourage you to do a little research and find an old-fashioned baking recipe, drink recipes, or a nice leg of lamb, and then share it with others at a group social event.

Travis I. Sivart

23. Community

The community of people in steampunk is one of the most welcoming and friendly groups I've ever met. I'm not saying everyone is going to greet you like an old friend, but more often than not, the creative folks drawn to steampunk are open to exploring new things. This includes friendships. They're looking for a new way to do things by embracing old things, and this encourages old-fashioned manners and behaviors. Steampunks pull from the best of both worlds.

Small local groups abound and many have regular get-togethers, usually about once a month. They do craft afternoons, meals at restaurants, movie going experiences in full garb, museum trips, picnics, sight-seeing, and so much more. If you can't find a local group, perhaps it's time to start one.

On a national, or even global, scale there's a vast variety of ways to interact with other steampunk enthusiasts. Weekend long conventions, indie band performances, cruises, and train rides are just a few of the amazing group activities you can find.

Online groups are the easiest way to get started, and they're ripe with friendly folks that are eager to share their passion for steampunk.

Travis I. Sivart

24. Steampunk in Modern Pop Culture

Steampunk has existed even before it was named, but since it gained its own identity, it's blossomed.

Dozens of new books come out every year, and many authors have a magnificent series of books based in their own steampunk worlds, myself included. Comics have brought in steampunk influences, and many are set in a world full of gears, cogs, mad scientists, and intrepid explorers with that mid to late 1800s feel.

Movies and TV have also embraced it, giving cameos to steampunk or making an entire story around it. A simple google search will turn up a dozen television series and hundreds of movies that can help you enjoy steampunk in the comfort of your own home.

Don't forget to look online for this as well. YouTube has complete series you can watch with the click of a mouse. Online comics, fan fiction, and endless other entertainments await your perusal.

Travis I. Sivart

25. Music

Music has embraced steampunk because it isn't a genre on its own, but rather allows any genre of music to use steampunk components to enhance individual songs, entire albums, or build a band around the theme.

Many will argue that there isn't one type of music that is steampunk, and I would agree. But I would add that there are bands that do only steampunk. This may be by fashion or style, the feel of industrialization or hope in their sound, or by playing their own music to a steampunk crowd exclusively. I've seen rock, metal, pop, folk, punk, swing, big band, marching band, cabaret, and many other types of music that just sings steampunk when you hear it!

Travis I. Sivart

26. Meeting Others

The hardest part of any hobby is meeting others. This is a bit easier once you know where to look, and steampunk is no different. It's pretty easy to find groups on social media like Facebook.com, or on social websites like Meetup.com.

A quick search of your area will reveal full day events, from picnics, historic walks, movie premieres, or just gatherings in general. There are also weekend long conventions spread throughout the world.

Another option is to just have your own steampunk party. This can be an afternoon tea, a poker game, a backyard barbeque, or just a get together with your friends. Don't be afraid to put something together yourself or with a few like-minded folks.

27. You Can't Do It Wrong

I tell folks the only way to do steampunk wrong is by telling others they are doing it wrong. Steampunk is a very individualistic thing. Though we may get new ideas from others, even copy elements of bands, movies, books, history, or friends, we all set our own style in steampunk.

I encourage you to embrace individuality and beware conformity. Steampunk is not about being like everyone else, it's about being who you are in a way that you enjoy blended with this historical influence and fictional flair. Whether you cobble everything together, or buy every single thing you use and wear in steampunk, it's still steampunk.

Come on out and enjoy!

Travis I. Sivart

About the Author

Travis I. Sivart lives in a state of constant flux between Richmond, VA and Washington, DC with his son and cats. He is not just an author but also a father, public speaker, cook, pipe smoker, cat & squirrel lover, internet radio host, and so much more.

Travis I. Sivart is a Jack-Of-All-Trades. He has worked in mundane jobs such as restaurants, retail, construction, DMV, notary, tech help, and more…as well as more exotic trades such as; singing pirate, exorcist and paranormal researcher, Duke, cigar and pipe connoisseur, master of dungeons, a knight, therapist, minister, King, and has degrees in religion and metaphysics.

Travis I. Sivart writes steampunk, social DIY, science fiction, fantasy, young adult, speculative fiction, horror, and more.

You can find Travis at www.TravisISivart.com.

Travis I. Sivart

If you enjoyed this book…

Please let others know by reviewing it on Amazon or Goodreads, and let others know your thoughts!

Other books by Travis I. Sivart:

<u>Aetheric Elements: The Rise of a Steampunk Reality</u>

Automatons and airships, bustles and beasts, corsets and curses, dandies and dastardly deeds, all await you as you explore the cultures which evolved into a Steampunk industrial civilization. An anthology of nineteen tales of terror, mystery, and adventure.

<u>Steampunk For Simpletons: A Fun Primer For Folks Who Aren't Sure What Steampunk Is All About</u>

A primer followed by a guided tour through the world of steampunk, from the basics such as where to go and what to do, to the aesthetic of the arts within steampunk.

<u>Journal of a Stranger</u>

The thoughts, ideas, philosophies, and inspirations of a time traveling adventurer. Delving into the psychology of man, life's eternal questions, burning passions, and the quirky pseudo-science of his mind, and more.

<u>The Downfall: Harbinger</u>

The Talisman came again, but this time it didn't leave. The magical emanations of the comet have brought terrors from the bowels of the earth and increased the powers of an insane necromancer. The chaos above brought out others seeking to wrest control of the land. Five people from different walks of life are thrown together by these events with the knowledge that the world as they know it is ending.

Travis I. Sivart

27 Thoughts About Steampunk

Travis I. Sivart